Group resources actually work!

This Group resource helps you focus on **"The 1 Thing™"**— a life-changing relationship with Jesus Christ. "The 1 Thing" incorporates our **R.E.A.L.** approach to ministry. It reinforces a growing friendship with Jesus, encourages long-term learning, and results in life transformation, because it's:

Relational
Learner-to-learner interaction enhances learning and builds Christian friendships.

Experiential
What learners experience through discussion and action sticks with them up to 9 times longer than what they simply hear or read.

Applicable
The aim of Christian education is to equip learners to be both hearers and doers of God's Word.

Learner-based
Learners understand and retain more when the learning process takes into consideration how they learn best.

Coloring Creations: 52 Bible Activity Pages

Copyright © 2005 Group Publishing, Inc.

Visit our Web site: **www.group.com**

Credits
Authors: Heather A. Eades, Sharon Carey, Laurie Castañeda, Teryl Cartwright, Ruthie Daniels, Marsha Hall, Larry Shallenberger, and Bonnie Temple
Senior Editor: Mikal Keefer
Editor: Roxanne Wieman
Copy Editor: Christy Fagerlin
Chief Creative Officer: Joani Schultz
Art Director: Randy Kady
Print Production Artist: Greg Longbons, Coffee Bean Design Company
Cover Art Director/Designer: Bambi Eitel
Production Manager: Peggy Naylor

Unless otherwise noted, Scripture taken from the HOLY BIBLE, NEW INTERNATIONAL VERSION®. Copyright © 1973, 1978, 1984 by International Bible Society. Used by permission of Zondervan Publishing House. All rights reserved.

Library of Congress Cataloging-in-Publication Data

Coloring creations : 52 Bible activity pages.-- 1st American pbk. ed.
    p. cm.
  Includes indexes.
  ISBN 0-7644-2767-9 (pbk. : alk. paper)
 1. Bible crafts. 2. Church work with children. 3. Christian education--Activity programs. I. Group Publishing.
  BS613.C57 2004
  268'.432--dc22
                        2004013043

ISBN 0-7644-2767-9
10 9 8 7 6 5 4 3   07 06
Printed in the United States of America.

Contents

Introduction

The sermon runs long. The lesson runs short. Your preschoolers are running all over the place.

Sometimes those days just happen. You've used every activity in the book, and the clock still says you have ten minutes of class left. It's Easter Sunday, and you have twice as many kids as usual and only half as many supplies. Your kids are losing interest in the lesson, and you desperately want to get them back. Children's ministry is full of twists and turns, ups and downs. It doesn't always go the way you think it will, and sometimes you need a new and innovative...and fast...idea in your classroom.

So here it is: Coloring Creations: *52 Bible Activity Pages*, the perfect book for anyone who has ever experienced "one of those days" in children's ministry. Coloring Creations looks like a coloring book, but it's more than just a coloring book. It's an activity page book. Each reproducible coloring page is accompanied by a relevant *B*ible story and Scripture verse, an activity to make the page 3-D, and an age-appropriate discussion guide to help you make the activity applicable and relevant for your students. Each activity in this book is a chance for you to expand on a lesson, dig a little deeper into a theme or topic, and teach a valuable lesson to your students.

The pages in this book are repro*du***cib***l***e,** so the book belongs on your bookshelf where it can be pulled out and used again and again—for years.

Ea*c***h a***c***tivity is base***d* **on a Bib***l***e story,** which makes this book a wonderful tool for any children's ministry leader. Simply locate the activity page in this book that best accompanies the story you're teaching and you've got an instant enhancement for your lesson. The page will give you another opportunity for teaching the *B*ible story, as well as giving kids a fun craft activity that they can take home.

Ea*c***h page a***l***so emphasizes a theme or point.** This point is introduced through a Scripture verse, then continued in the activity and the discussion section. These central points or themes are focused on life application; they offer the children a way to live out the lesson of the *B*ible story. If children are discovering the story of the good Samaritan, they will learn to care for each other. If they hear the story of how Esther saved her people, they will understand that God has special plans for their lives.

Ea*c***h c***o***loring page is more than a c***o***loring page:** it's a 3-D, multisensory, supertactile creation! Your kids will color the page...decorate it, cut it, fold it, paint it, and all around change it.

Ea*c***h page is a***cc***ompanie***d* **by instru***c***tions** to help you turn pictures into 3-D masterpieces that help kids learn and remember the *B*ible story and the theme. The instructions are simple, the supplies general, and the process rewarding. You won't just be adding stuff to be adding stuff either; each piece of the craft means something and will help you further enhance the lesson for your kids.

We know that sometimes coloring has been considered a simple time-stuffing activity. Well, no more! Coloring Creations can help you transform coloring time into relationship time...and teaching time, too. With this book, coloring becomes more than mere busywork—it's a chance to engage your children in dialogue, to grow deeper relationships, and to teach lasting *B*ible truths!

Now you no longer have to fear those days when class feels like it will never end. Just grab this book off your shelf, use the indexes to locate the activity page that best fits your lesson, make a copy of the page for each child, gather the necessary supplies...and get started on an activity that will help your children grow in their relationships with Jesus!

Coloring Creations Kit

Many of the coloring pages in this book use basic supplies to transform the pages into craft projects kids love. Take a few moments to gather the following supplies and place them in a plastic box to use with this book. That way you will always have the right supplies available at a moment's notice.

Tuck these items in your "Coloring Creations Kit":

- craft glue
- glue sticks
- crayons
- markers
- colored pencils
- tape
- safety scissors

When you see, "remember to bring your Coloring Creations Kit!" in a supply list, you'll know the basic supplies are already gathered and ready to use!

Allergy Alert! Some of the projects in this book involve food. Be aware that some children have food allergies that can be dangerous. Know your children, and consult with parents about allergies their children may have. Also be sure to carefully read food labels, as hidden ingredients can cause allergy-related problems.

Choking Hazards! Be aware that small objects can be choking hazards for younger children. Supervise children as they work with small objects such as buttons, dry cereal, and googley eyes. If you have several young children in your class, you may want to substitute a larger object for the craft.

God Creates the World

Genesis 1:1–2:22

What you need:

For each child...

• 1 copy of page 7

You'll also need...

• black, yellow, red, and brown yarn;
• black construction paper;
• small silk flowers and leaves (optional);
  and remember to bring your
• Coloring Creations Kit!

What to do:

Write children's names on their pages. Cut black construction paper into small pieces (approximately ½x½-inch); provide enough for each child to thinly cover his or her picture.

1. Give each child an activity page. Ask children to look at the picture and name some things God created.

2. Have children put a small dot of glue on several of the giraffe's spots, then help children sprinkle a thin layer of the black paper scraps over their pictures to make them dark. Remind kids that before God made everything, the world did not exist, and all was dark and black.

3. Ask children to place their hands on their pictures and press down firmly as they say the Scripture verse together. Explain how God spoke, and the world was created. Let children shake off loose scraps of paper from their pages until the only scraps remaining are pieces stuck onto the spots of the giraffe.

4. After children have colored the pictures, have each child choose yarn the color of his or her hair and glue the yarn over Adam's and Eve's hair.

5. If time allows, encourage children to glue small silk leaves and flowers on their pictures. Encourage children to show the "God Creates the World" activity page to their families and thank God for his wonderful creation.

Talk about:

Ask: • What are some of your favorite things that God created?

• How can you thank God for creating the world?

Say: Our God is the great Creator, and we can praise God for all he has made. We can enjoy things God has made: we can play outside, we can drink cool water, and we can spend time with our families and friends. God made all those things, and it makes God happy when we are enjoying his creations. Let's thank God for all the wonderful things he made!

Pray: Lord, you are a great God who makes wonderful things. Thank you for creating me and everything my eyes can see. In Jesus' name, amen.

"In the beginning God created the heavens and the earth"

(Genesis 1:1).

Noah's Ark

Genesis 6:5-22; 7:1–8:22; 9:8-16

What you need:

For each child...
- 1 copy of page 9
- 1 foam or paper bowl
- animal crackers

You'll also need...
- your Coloring Creations Kit!

What to do:

Write children's names on their pages. Set all the items except the animal crackers out on the table.

1. Tell children that after coloring their pictures, they will help Noah get the ark ready to add the rest of the animals that haven't arrived yet.

2. Set out the animal crackers, and let each child choose two or three crackers to glue to their pages. As children work, tell kids that God told Noah to build a great, big ark to put all the animals in. The ark was like a boat, and it would keep the animals safe when God flooded the Earth. Noah was careful to follow all God's instructions.

3. As kids finish their pictures, tell children to listen carefully to your instructions so that their arks will turn out well, just like the one Noah built. Show children how to prop their picture up around the inside of a paper bowl and tape it in place. Cut a small opening for a door somewhere above the edges of the bowl on each child's paper.

4. When everyone is finished, give each child a serving of animal crackers and have them "walk" the animals through the door and into the ark. Invite one child to thank God for the food, and then let kids enjoy the snack! Be sure to check your children for food allergies.

Talk about:

Ask:
- **How did God take care of Noah and the animals?**
- **How did Noah follow God?**
- **How can you follow God?**

Say: God told Noah what to do to be safe from the flood. Noah obeyed God and followed all his instructions. The Bible tells us that God wants us to obey our moms and dads when we're little. So when you obey your parents, you're obeying God and following him, just like Noah did!

Pray: Dear God, thank you for taking care of Noah and all the animals. Help us to follow you too, just like Noah did. In Jesus' name, amen.

"Obey the Lord your God with all your heart"
(adapted from Deuteronomy 30:2).

Abram and Sarai Begin to Pack

Genesis 12:1-8

What you need:

For each child...

- 1 copy of page 11
- one 4x4-inch piece of fabric
- 2 craft sticks
- cereal pieces

You'll also need...

- sand or gold glitter, and remember to bring your
- Coloring Creations Kit!

What to do:

Write children's names on their pages. Cut fabric scraps about four inches square to match the tent size on the activity page.

1. Give each child an activity page, and encourage kids to begin coloring. As children work, explain that God told Abram and Sarai to leave the land where they lived and move to a new and better place. Abram loved God and was happy to obey God's rules. God blessed Abram and Sarai with many riches because of his obedience. Abram was happy because he obeyed God and God blessed him.

2. Point out that, in the picture, Abram and Sarai are packing for their long trip—they even had to fold up their huge tent! Explain to children that they'll help Abram and Sarai roll up the tent. Help children glue just the top of their fabric square to the top of the tent on the activity page, and then glue a craft stick on top of that. Next, have children glue another craft stick to the bottom, loose end of the fabric. Show children how to roll the fabric around the craft stick until the tent is all rolled up!

3. When children are finished, have them glue several pieces of cereal onto the bread in the basket and some gold glitter or sand onto the ground.

4. As children work, remind them that they can obey God and follow him just as Abram and Sarai followed God. Encourage children to show their "Abram and Sarai Begin to Pack" activity pages to their families as a reminder that everyone can have faith in and obey God.

Talk about:

Ask: • **Have you ever had to move? What did you pack?**

• **How did Abram and Sarai follow God?**

• **What are some things that God asks us to do?**

Say: **We can follow God by obeying our parents, being nice to others, sharing our things, and by following what our teachers or grandparents tell us to do.**

Pray: **Dear Lord, help us to follow you in all that we do. In Jesus' name, amen.**

"By faith, Abraham obeyed God"
(adapted from Hebrews 11:8).

Abraham and Lot

Genesis 13:1-18

What you need:

For each child...
- 1 copy of page 13

You'll also need...
- cotton balls, and remember to bring your
- Coloring Creations Kit!

What to do:

Write children's names on their pages. Set out cotton balls and glue sticks.

1. Give each child a copy of the "Abraham and Lot" activity page. Have children color their pictures.

2. When children are finished coloring, divide them into pairs, and give each pair a pile of cotton balls and two glue sticks. Have kids take turns pulling apart the cotton balls, gluing half on their sheep and then giving the other half to their partners to glue on their pictures.

3. Tell kids that Abraham loved Lot and let him choose the land he wanted. Remind children that Abraham was thinking of Lot first and what would make Lot happy. Encourage children to show their "Abraham and Lot" activity pages to their families as a reminder that everyone should think of others first.

Talk about:

Ask: • **How do you think Abraham felt when he was sharing with Lot?**

• **How do you think it made Lot feel?**

• **When you were sharing the cotton balls with your partner, how did you feel?**

Say: **Abraham loved God very much and knew how happy it made God when he put others first. Abraham let Lot choose which piece of land Lot wanted, and Abraham took the other piece without complaining. Have you ever let someone choose something before you? Maybe you let them choose first which cookie or toy they wanted.**
God wants each of us to put others first.
It makes God happy when we think of others and put them first.

Pray: **Lord, help us to think of others first and to share with them. In Jesus' name, amen.**

"Be devoted to one another in brotherly love. Honor one another above yourselves"

(Romans 12:10).

God Gives Abraham and Sarah a Child

Genesis 21:1-6

What you need:

For each child...

• 1 copy of page 15
• lemon slice candy (if you can't find this candy, use red chenille wire bent into the shape of a smile)
• small square of felt

You'll also need...

• your Coloring Creations Kit!

What to do:

Write children's names on their pages. Set out the glue, lemon slice candy, felt squares, and crayons or markers.

1. Give each child a copy of the activity page and several crayons or markers. Give kids some time to color in the pages.

2. Show children how to glue candy smiles on Abraham's and Sarah's faces to show how happy they were. Explain that Abraham and Sarah weren't always happy. For a long time, they wanted a baby to love—but they couldn't have one. God promised to give Sarah a baby, but Sarah was so old that it didn't seem possible. God was faithful though and gave them what he had promised; Abraham and Sarah had a little baby boy!

3. Have children glue a felt square on the baby's body as a blanket. Remind the kids that God loves them, and he will always be faithful to them and care for them; they can trust God to keep his promises, just as Abraham and Sarah trusted God for a baby. Encourage children to show the "God Gives Abraham and Sarah a Baby" activity page to their families as a reminder that God always keeps his promises.

Talk about:

Ask: • **How do you think Abraham and Sarah felt when God gave them their baby?**

• **What do you think they said to God?**

• **Has God ever kept a promise he made to you? How did you feel?**

Say: **Abraham and Sarah were happy because God kept his promise to them. God makes promises to us too. God promises to love and protect us. We can trust God to keep those promises to us, just as he kept his promise to Abraham and Sarah.**

Pray: **God, thank you for keeping your promises to us. Because you keep your promises, we are your happy people. In Jesus' name, amen.**

"Bring joy to your servant, O Lord"
(Psalm 86:4a).

God Protects Baby Moses

Exodus 1:1–2:10

What you need:

For each child...
- 1 copy of page 17
- 10 wide blades of grass or green curly ribbon

You'll also need...
- your Coloring Creations Kit!

What to do:

Write children's names on their pages. Cut about ten wide blades of grass for each child in your class. Don't forget a few extras for visitors. If you can't use real grass, use green curly ribbon or shredded green paper.

1. Give each child an activity page. Read the Bible verse to children, and point out the basket and grass around the riverbank. Tell the kids that Moses' mom hid him in the basket among the tall grass that grew at the edge of the river. God used the grass and basket to protect baby Moses from the mean Pharaoh who wanted to kill Moses.

2. Provide crayons, liquid glue, and grass. Have children color their activity page first so the glue won't ruin the crayons or markers.

3. Show children how to carefully squeeze a line of glue just below the bottom of the basket and place several blades of grass over the line of glue. As children work, remind them God is our hiding place and will protect us, just as he protected baby Moses. Encourage children to show their "God Protects Baby Moses" activity page to their families as a reminder that God protects us.

Talk about:

Ask:
- **Where is baby Moses hiding?**
- **How did God protect baby Moses?**
- **What things do you hide from?**

Say: When we're afraid, we can ask God to protect us and be our hiding place. When danger is over, we can celebrate and sing for joy because God has kept his promise and protected us.

Pray: Dear Lord, thank you for being my hiding place. Thank you for protecting me and keeping me safe. In Jesus' name, amen.

"You are my hiding place; you will protect me from trouble"

(Psalm 32:7a).

Permission to photocopy this coloring page from *Coloring Creations: 52 Bible Activity Pages* granted for local church use. Copyright © Group Publishing, Inc., P.O. Box 481, Loveland, CO 80539. www.grouppublishing.com

God Comforts the Israelites

Exodus 5:1–6:1

What you need:

For each child...

- 1 copy of page 19
- 5 small brown fun-foam rectangles
- 3 spaghetti noodles
- 1 teaspoon of coffee grounds

You'll also need...

- your Coloring Creations Kit!

What to do:

Write children's names on their pages. Cut the brown fun-foam into small pieces of bricks to match the bricks on the activity page. Cut about five for each of your children. Each child will also need three spaghetti noodles, broken into one-inch pieces.

1. Give each child an activity page. Encourage kids to begin coloring their pages. Read the Bible verse to the children. Remind children that the Israelites put their hope in God when they were slaves in Egypt. The Israelites knew God loved them and would take care of them. Even though the Israelites had to work hard as slaves, they knew God would keep his promise and give them their own land someday. And God did keep his promise! We can put our hope in God too. God always keeps his promises to us.

2. Give children the fun-foam bricks, spaghetti pieces, coffee grounds, and liquid glue. Help children glue foam bricks over the bricks on the picture and noodle pieces over some of the straw.

3. Help children squeeze glue over parts of the straw and then sprinkle coffee grounds on the glue to look like mud. Shake excess into the trash. Tell the children the Israelites had to mix straw and mud together to make bricks. As children work, remind them that we can put our hope in God, just as the Israelites did. Encourage the children to show their "God Comforts the Israelites" activity pages to their families as a reminder that we can put our hope in God.

Talk about:

Ask: • **What was the hard thing that Pharaoh made the Israelites do?**

• **What are some hard things you have to do?**

• **How can our God help you be happy even when you have to do something hard?**

Say: Praying and talking to God when we feel sad is one way God's love helps us to be happy during hard times. If we put our hope in God, we can know that God will help us and take care of us.

Pray: Dear Lord, thank you for your love that never stops. When we go through hard times, help us put our hope in you. In Jesus' name, amen.

"Hope in the Lord"
(Isaiah 40:31a).

The Exodus: Leaving Egypt

Exodus 12:31-42

What you need:

For each child...

- 1 copy of page 21
- 1 teddy-bear sticker or other baby-toy sticker

You'll also need...

- a variety of small, dried food items such as cereal, oyster crackers, raisins, macaroni, or dried beans;
- chocolate chips;
- white chocolate chips (optional); and remember to bring your
- Coloring Creations Kit!

What to do:

Write children's names on their pages.

1. Give each child an activity page, and set out the other items. Tell children they are going to help this family pack their things to leave Egypt. Explain that God's people had been forced to be slaves to the Pharaoh for 400 years. Now God was going to save the Israelites and lead them out of Egypt.

2. Ask children what they think each family member in the picture might want to take on the long trip. Remind the children the Israelites had to pack in a hurry and probably had to leave many things behind.

3. Give each child a toy sticker to place near the baby and dry food to glue in the baskets on the donkey.

4. Ask the kids what they think the child in the picture had wrapped in his blanket. Have the children draw their answer somewhere on the page. Then have the kids draw something that they would take on a big trip.

5. Give each child several chocolate chips. Be sure to check for food allergies. Allow the kids to eat a few, and then show them that they can use a chocolate chip to color the donkey! Encourage them to smell the donkey—a donkey never smelled that good! If you want, give the kids white chocolate chips to color the sheep. Encourage children to show the "Exodus: Leaving Egypt" page to their families as a reminder that God saves us.

Talk about:

Ask: • How did God save the Israelites?

• Have you ever had to move? Tell us about it.

• How did God help you when you moved?

Say: God gives us moms and dads to take care of us when we're small, just like the kids in the picture. It's great to know that God saves us from bad things. He loves us and protects us.

Pray: Thank you, God, for saving us. Help us to always trust you. In Jesus' name, amen.

"The Lord will save us"

(adapted from Isaiah 33:22).

Crossing the Red Sea

Exodus 13:17–14:31

What you need:

For each child...
• 1 copy of page 23
• cotton swab

You'll also need...
• paintbrushes,
• coffee grounds,
• a shallow pan of water,
• blue watercolor paint, and remember to bring your
• Coloring Creations Kit!

What to do:

Write children's names on their pages. Set out a shallow pan of water.

1. Give each child a paintbrush. Ask the children to try and move their paintbrushes through the water without getting them wet. The kids will soon realize you have asked them to do something impossible. Remind the children of the very special way God took care of the Israelites when he helped them leave Egypt.

2. Give each child an activity page, and explain how God pulled back the water of the Red Sea and let all the people walk through the sea on dry ground. Let children color Moses and the Israelites.

3. Encourage each child to use the paintbrush and paint the waves with blue watercolor paint.

4. Invite children to use a cotton swab to spread a light coat of glue on the sand in the picture. Let kids sprinkle dry coffee grounds over the glue to resemble the dry ground on which the Israelites walked.

Encourage the children to show the "Crossing the Red Sea" activity page to their families as a reminder to them that God cares for his people.

Talk about:

Ask: • How did God take care of the Israelites?

• How has God taken care of you in the past?

Say: It was impossible for the Israelites to cross the Red Sea on dry ground, but God took care of them. God brought the Israelites safely out of Egypt and gave the Israelites a new home. God knows what we need and God takes care of us. God gives us food, clothing, and a home in which to live. God keeps us safe and helps us live for him.

Pray: Lord, thank you for knowing what I need and for caring for me. Help me to trust you when I need help. In Jesus' name, amen.

"Cast all your anxiety on him because he cares for you"
(1 Peter 5:7).

Permission to photocopy this coloring page from *Coloring Creations: 52 Bible Activity Pages* granted for local church use. Copyright © Group Publishing, Inc., P.O. Box 481, Loveland, CO 80539. www.grouppublishing.com

God Gives Us Good Things

Exodus 16:1-26

What you need:

For each child...

• 1 copy of page 25

You'll also need...

• age-appropriate magazines, and remember to bring your
• Coloring Creations Kit!

What to do:

Write children's names on their pages. Set out the magazines and several glue sticks.

1. Hand out the activity pages, and encourage children to begin coloring them. If you have scented crayons or markers, this would be a great opportunity to use them!

2. When children finish coloring, have them look through the magazines and tear or cut out pictures of things for which they are thankful. Remind kids God gives them such good things. Everything good they see comes from God.

3. Tell children to glue pictures from the magazines onto the plate in the picture. As children work, talk with them about different things they are thankful for, and encourage them to pray and thank God for the many good things God has given them. Remind children that everything good they find in the magazine is a gift from God. Encourage children to show the "God Gives Us Good Things" activity page to their families as a reminder that God provides us with all the good things in our life.

Talk about:

Ask: • What are some things you are thankful for?

• Who are some people you are thankful for? Why?

• What would your life be like if you didn't have these things?

Say: We thank God for loving us so much and for taking care of us. This picture you are making can help you remember some of the things you can thank God for each day. When you look at this picture, you can think about how much God loves you, and you can thank God for the wonderful things he has given you.

Pray: Lord, thank you for loving us and taking care of us. Thank you for all the people and things you've given us. In Jesus' name, amen.

"Give thanks to the Lord...for he satisfies the thirsty and fills the hungry with good things" (Psalm 107:8-9).

Moses Strikes the Rock, and God Provides Water

Exodus 17:1-7

What you need:

For each child...

- 1 copy of page 27
- 1 cotton swab
- 8-ounce foam cup

You'll also need...

- water,
- blue food coloring, and remember to bring your
- Coloring Creations Kit!

What to do:

Write children's names on their pages. Ahead of time, tint the glue with blue food coloring.

1. Let kids name things God has provided for them. When the kids mention water, give each of them a foam cup of water. Let kids drink the water and then scribble color on the outside of their cups with brown or black crayons.

2. Give each child an activity page and encourage them to color the page. Remind children of the time when God provided water from a rock for the people of Israel. The people were very thirsty, and they couldn't find water anywhere. God told Moses to strike the rock, and when Moses did, God provided water from the rock!

3. After kids have colored the picture, have children break their foam cups into small (approximately one-inch) pieces. Encourage kids to glue these small "rocks" onto the mountain in their pictures.

4. With the cotton swabs, have children lightly paint the tinted glue onto the water flowing from the mountain. When the glue dries, it will remain shiny. Encourage children to show the "Moses Strikes the Rock, and God Provides Water" activity page to their families as a reminder that God will always provide for his people and meet their needs.

Talk about:

Ask:
- **In what ways does God provide for us every day?**
- **What is the greatest thing God has given you?**
- **How can you show thankfulness for the things God provides?**

Say: **God provides all that we need. Every day God gives us food, clothing, and a warm place to live. Most of all, God has given us love. We can say thank you to God by sharing what he has given us with others and by taking good care of the things God gives us.**

Pray: **Lord, thank you for giving me** [have the children name something God has provided for them]. **In Jesus' name, amen.**

"I provide water in the desert"

(Isaiah 43:20b).

The Ten Commandments

Exodus 19:16–20:21

What you need:

For each child...

- 1 copy of page 29
- 1 cotton ball

You'll also need...

- 1 roll of aluminum foil,
- sand in a saltshaker, and remember to bring your
- Coloring Creations Kit!

What to do:

Write children's names on their pages. Fill a saltshaker with sand. Set out the saltshaker, cotton balls, and aluminum foil.

1. Give each child an activity page. Let kids follow a simple rule such as coloring only the rocks in their picture and then placing their crayons down on top of their pages.

2. When the kids follow this command, explain that God has also given us important rules to follow and obey. Remind the children that Moses was given the Ten Commandments to help everyone know how to obey God. Show kids where the Ten Commandments are found in the Bible (Exodus 20), and give a simple summary of the commandments.

3. Ask kids to follow some more "activity page commandments." Instruct children by saying: "Spread glue on the picture of the stone tablets. Now shake a little bit of sand over the glue." Continue to instruct children this way as they color and decorate their pages. Have kids glue cotton on the clouds and on the beard of Moses. Then, encourage children to add strips of foil to the lightning bolts.

4. When the picture is finished, praise children for their good work, and thank kids for following your instructions. Encourage them to share the "Ten Commandments" activity page with their families and display it at home as a reminder to obey God every day.

Talk about:

Ask: • **Why was it important to follow my instructions for decorating your pages?**

  • **Why is it important to obey God's commands?**

  • **How can you obey God today?**

Say: **By following my instructions, we had fun, and all your pages look beautiful! Following God is even more important. God gives us commands in the Bible to help us know what is right and wrong. When we obey God's rules we please God, and pleasing God makes us happy.**

Pray: **Lord, thank you for helping us know what is right and wrong. Help us to obey you every day. In Jesus' name, amen.**

"Keep [the Lord your God's] commands and obey him"
(Deuteronomy 13:4b).

The Walls Came Tumbling Down

Joshua 6:1-27

What you need:

For each child...

- 1 copy of page 31
- 10 to 15 mini marshmallows

You'll also need...

- your Coloring Creations Kit!

What to do:

Write children's names on their pages.

1. Give each child an activity page and crayons or markers. Encourage the kids to begin coloring their pages. Read the Bible verse to children, and tell them that God is powerful enough to make huge walls fall down at the sound of his voice. Remind children that the Israelites marched around the city of Jericho seven times, then the Israelites blew their trumpets, shouted loudly, and watched as God made the walls tumble down. God's voice is powerful, and God won the victory for the Israelites!

2. When kids have finished coloring the pages, explain that you want the kids to retell the Bible story by stacking their mini marshmallows like a wall on their activity pages where they see the falling stones.

3. Encourage kids to pretend to blow trumpets by placing their hands around their mouths. Have children stomp their feet and shout really loudly. Then, encourage kids to blow down their marshmallow walls.

4. When the marshmallows fall, have kids use thick craft glue to glue the marshmallows where they fell on the picture. As children work, remind them that the walls of Jericho came tumbling down after the Israelites obeyed God and listened to God's powerful voice. Encourage children to show their "Walls Came Tumbling Down" activity page to their families as a reminder that God is powerful.

Talk about:

Ask: • What did God tell the Israelites to do?

• What do you think God's powerful voice sounds like?

• What powerful things do you think God can do in your life?

Say: God can do many powerful things. God can make the earth shake, thunder crash, and walls tumble. Just as God was powerful when he made the walls of Jericho come tumbling down, God is still powerful today.

Pray: Dear Lord, you are the most powerful of all. Thank you for doing powerful things for the Israelites a long time ago and for me today. I love you. In Jesus' name, amen.

"The voice of the Lord is powerful"
(Psalm 29:4a).

Ruth and Boaz

Ruth 2–4

What you need:

For each child...

- 1 copy of page 33
- heart stickers

You'll also need...

- tinted makeup such as blush;
- cotton swabs;
- food coloring;
- small bowls or paper cups;
- water;
- decorative items such as sequins, glitter, and ribbon;
- scented liquid extracts such as vanilla or almond; and remember to bring your
- Coloring Creations Kit!

What to do:

Write children's names on their pages. Put some food coloring in small, individual containers such as condiment bowls or small paper cups. Add a little bit of water to the cups to dilute the food coloring.

1. Give each child an activity page. Tell kids they'll help Ruth and Boaz prepare for their wedding! Briefly remind children that when Ruth was alone and had moved to a strange new place, Ruth trusted the Lord to take care of her. God sent Ruth a wonderful husband to love named Boaz.

2. Give each child a few cotton swabs, and have kids use the food coloring to "paint" Ruth's and Boaz's clothing. Remind kids to use a clean swab each time they change colors.

3. Encourage children to use ribbon, sequins, glitter and other craft supplies to finish decorating Ruth's and Boaz's clothes. Then show kids how to dab a little blush on Ruth's cheeks (they can also use red or pink crayon and then rub it with their fingers). As a finishing touch, allow children to dab a bit of the scented extract on the figures.

4. Finally, have kids decorate the page with hearts to show Ruth's and Boaz's love for one another and for God. As children work, remind them that Ruth put her hope in God and God provided for her. Have children take their activity pages home as a reminder that everyone can put their hope in God.

Talk about:

Ask:
- **How did God take care of Ruth?**
- **What things do you hope for?**
- **How has God taken care of you?**

Say: Ruth loved God and put her hope in God. God loved Ruth. God took care of Ruth and gave her a special person to love her and take care of her.

Pray: Thank you, Jesus, for caring about the things we need. Help us to put our hope in you. Help us to be like Ruth and trust you to take care of us. In Jesus' name, amen.

"Put your hope in God"
(Psalm 42:11b).

David and Goliath

1 Samuel 17:1-50

What you need:

For each child...

• 1 copy of page 35

You'll also need...

• silver or black sequins,
• masking tape,
• foil,
• brown yarn, and remember to bring your
• Coloring Creations Kit!

What to do:

Write children's names on their pages. Set out the sequins, foil, and yarn.

1. Give each child an activity page. Ask children to look at David and Goliath and describe the differences between the two men.

2. When kids mention Goliath's heavy armor, have children glue sequins onto Goliath's breastplate.

3. When kids compare David's slingshot and stones with Goliath's spear, have children tape one end of a two-inch piece of yarn onto the sling in David's hand. Show kids how to press a one-inch piece of masking tape into a ball with the sticky side out so that it resembles a rock. Encourage children to attach the "rock" to the "sling" and onto the activity page at an appropriate spot. Have kids shape a small piece of foil into a spearhead, and glue it onto the spear tip.

4. As children color the remaining parts of their pictures, remind kids that David was not afraid of Goliath because David knew he had God's help to do a great thing. Encourage children to show the "David and Goliath" activity page to their families and to share ways people can trust God to help them do great things.

Talk about:

Ask: • **How was David different from Goliath?**

• **What great thing did God help David do?**

• **What great things can God help you do?**

Say: **The mean giant, Goliath, was much bigger and stronger than David. God helped David defeat Goliath and show everyone that with God's help we can do great things. When we tell others about Jesus or when we are kind, we are doing great things for God—just like David.**

Pray: **Lord, help me to do great things for you! In Jesus' name, amen.**

"The Lord is my strength and my shield"
(Psalm 28:7a).

Friends Stick Together

1 Samuel 18:1-4; 19:1-7; 20:1-42

What you need:

For each child...

• 1 copy of page 37

You'll also need...

• clear packing tape, and remember to bring your
• Coloring Creations Kit!

What to do:

Write children's names on their pages.

1. Ask children to each find a friend and hold that friend's hand while you read the Bible verse. Remind children that a good friend is important to have.

2. Give each child an activity page and crayons or markers. Have kids look at the picture and tell you how they know that the girls in the picture are friends.

3. Have children color their papers. As kids work, tell the story of David and Jonathan. Remind children that good friends stick together and help each other.

4. Pair children so that each child can hold an end of a piece of packaging tape. Tell kids to take turns putting pieces of tape on each other's activity page until their pictures of the friends are covered with clear tape.

5. Ask children to try to color over the tape and change their pictures. Point out that the crayons can't color on the picture anymore now that the tape is on top. Encourage children to show the "Friends Stick Together" activity page to their families as a reminder that good friends stay close and help each other.

Talk about:

Ask: • **How do you find good friends?**

• **What makes someone a good friend?**

• **How can you be a good friend?**

Say: No matter what changes in your life, a good friend doesn't change. A good friend sticks close to you—like the tape sticks to the picture. A good friend is someone special. Look around you. You have many good friends here!

Pray: Dear God, thank you for giving us good friends to stick close to us. We are glad to have these special people with us. In Jesus' name, amen.

"But there is a friend who sticks closer than a brother"
(Proverbs 18:24b).

Help One Another

Exodus 31:1-11

What you need:

For each child...

- 1 copy of page 39
- seven 1-inch squares cut from multicolored index cards

You'll also need...

- your Coloring Creations Kit!

What to do:

Write children's names on their pages. Cut multicolored index cards into one-inch squares. Each child will need about seven squares.

1. Give each child an activity page, and encourage the children to color the page. Read the Bible story (from Exodus 31). Explain to the kids that the Israelites were building a big temple, or church, for the Lord. The Israelites all had to work together and help each other build the temple. Some of the Israelites were really good at using wood to build, others were good at sewing, and others were good at making things with metal. The Israelites each did the things that they were good at, and they helped each other to build the temple.

2. Point out the two girls on the activity page. Remind children of their classroom cleanup time. When the kids have a friend to help clean up, they have more fun, and they pick up more toys or books in less time.

3. Explain that children will drop their paper squares (books) on the "floor" of the activity page, and then pick the books up. Kids will glue some of the books in one girl's arms and some in the other girl's arms.

4. Help children to sort the colored books and give each of the girls in the picture half of the books. As children work, remind them that helping each other is always better than working alone because they can do things faster and have more fun. Encourage children to show their "Help One Another" activity pages to their families as a reminder to help one another.

Talk about:

Ask: • How have you helped someone else?

• How did you feel after you helped that person?

• What are some different ways you can help others?

Say: God wants us to help one another so we can do more fun things. When we have a friend to help clean up, it's more fun, and we can pick up more toys or books in less time.

Pray: Dear Lord, help me to help all my friends so we can have more fun. Thank you for helping us too. In Jesus' name, amen.

"Two are better than one, because they have a good return for their work"

(Ecclesiastes 4:9).

Permission to photocopy this coloring page from *Coloring Creations: 52 Bible Activity Pages* granted for local church use. Copyright © Group Publishing, Inc., P.O. Box 481, Loveland, CO 80539. www.grouppublishing.com

God Provides in Amazing Ways for the Widow and Her Sons

2 Kings 4:1-7

What you need:

For each child...
- 1 copy of page 41

You'll also need...
- tempera paint,
- plastic straws,
- paint dishes,
- plastic spoons, and remember to bring your
- Coloring Creations Kit!

What to do:

Write children's names on their pages. Set out small dishes of tempera paint with a plastic spoon in each dish.

1. Give each child an activity page. Have children first color the page using crayons. Then remind students that Elisha helped the widow learn that God can provide everything we need—and he can do it in amazing ways. Explain that children are going to show how God can take something very tiny and make it grow, just as he did with the widow's oil.

2. Instruct children to spoon a tiny blob of paint onto the middle of their pages. Then give children each a straw, and have kids gently blow the paint around their pages. Help kids turn their pages in different directions so they can blow the paint to different areas.

3. As children work, remind them that even when things seem totally impossible, God can do amazing things to provide for them. Encourage children to show their "God Provides in Amazing Ways for the Widow and Her Sons" activity page to their families as a reminder to trust God to provide in amazing and wonderful ways.

Talk about:

Ask: • Did you think that your tiny blob of paint would be enough to cover the entire page? How did it make you feel when it did?

• How do you think the widow felt when Elisha helped her see God would give them enough food to eat?

• Has God given you something amazing? What is it?

• How can you remember to trust God for everything you need?

Say: God will always make sure that we have just what we need. It may look to us like we just don't have enough, but God loves us so much that he will always take care of us and do amazing things to make sure we have what we need.

Pray: God, thank you for loving us so much! You are such an amazing, awesome God! Help us to share with others so that they will have the things they need. We love you, God! In Jesus' name, amen.

"God will meet all your needs"
(adapted from Philippians 4:19).

God Heals Naaman's Leprosy

2 Kings 5:1-16

What you need:

For each child...

• 1 copy of page 43

You'll also need...

• watercolor paints,
• paintbrushes,
• water,
• water dishes,
• paper towels,

• small pieces of sponges (cut-up wedges),
• glue brushes,
• plastic Easter grass, and remember to bring your
• Coloring Creations Kit!

What to do:

Write children's names on their pages. Set out the watercolor paints, water dishes, and paintbrushes.

1. Give each child an activity page. Explain that kids are going to use the watercolors to paint the picture as a reminder of the water that Naaman bathed in. Remind kids that Naaman had leprosy—a very terrible disease. Have children paint red dots all over Naaman.

2. Explain that the prophet Elisha told Naaman to wash himself seven times in the Jordan River. Then God would make his sores all better, and he would be healed of leprosy. When Naaman bathed in the river, his sores were gone, just as Elisha had told him!

3. Have children each take a small piece of sponge and wipe off the spots from Naaman's body.

4. Encourage children to use the watercolor paints to finish coloring the rest of the picture, including Naaman. As children work, remind them that God can heal us just as God healed Naaman. God can make sick people well, God can heal our feelings and help us to feel better, God can heal our hearts when we our sad, and he can help us forgive someone by healing our anger and pain.

5. Once children are finished painting, have them use glue brushes to spread glue around the edges of the water in the picture. Then tell kids to press plastic Easter grass onto the glue. Encourage children to show their "God Heals Naaman's Leprosy" activity page to their families as a reminder that God can heal us.

Talk about:

Ask: • **Have you ever been really sick before? What was it like? How did you feel?**

• **How did you feel when you finally got better?**

• **How do you think Naaman must have felt to be clean from his disease?**

• **How has God healed you or someone you know?**

Say: God can heal us just like God healed Naaman. God can make sick people better, and God can heal our hearts and our feelings too. There isn't anything God can't do!

Pray: God, you are such an awesome God! We thank you that you are so powerful and strong and that you can heal us in many different ways. We love you, God! In Jesus' name, amen.

"For I am the Lord, who heals you"

(Exodus 15:26b).

Permission to photocopy this coloring page from *Coloring Creations: 52 Bible Activity Pages* granted for local church use. Copyright © Group Publishing, Inc., P.O. Box 481, Loveland, CO 80539. www.grouppublishing.com

Esther and the King

Esther 2–9

What you need:

For each child...

- 1 copy of page 45
- 1 craft stick

You'll also need...

- your Coloring Creations Kit!

What to do:

Write children's names on the top left and right of their pages.

1. Give each child an activity page and a pair of safety scissors. If your children are too young to use scissors, you will want to do this part before class. Have children cut Esther out of the larger picture by making a square around Esther—be sure to cut very close to Esther in order to leave as much room as possible between the left edge and the king.

2. Allow children to color their pictures. Remind kids that Esther went to the king and asked him to save her people. Explain to children that Esther could have gotten in trouble for talking to the king, but a friend told her she had to be brave in order to save her people. Read the Bible verse, and explain that sometimes God puts us in a certain place because God has a special plan for us to help him, just as Esther helped God in the story.

3. Have children tape the left end of a horizontal craft stick to the back, right side of the picture of Esther. Help children cut two vertical slits about an inch apart in the bottom left section of the picture of the king. Put tape on the sides of the slits so the slits don't rip wider.

4. Show kids how to weave the right end of the craft stick into the slots so when children pull the stick through the slots, Esther moves toward the king.

   Encourage children to show the "Esther and the King" activity page to their families as a reminder that, with God's help, we can be brave.

Talk about:

Ask: • What would you say to help a friend be brave?

• What do you say to yourself to help you do something you are scared to do?

Say: Esther's family and friends were in trouble, and she was the only person who could save them. Because Esther was brave and met with the king, she saved them.

Pray: God, help us to be brave when we need to be, and give us good friends to talk to when we are scared. In Jesus' name, amen.

"And who knows but that you have come to royal position for such a time as this?"

(Esther 4:14b).

Fiery Furnace

Daniel 3:1-30

What you need:

For each child...

• 1 copy of page 47

You'll also need...

• packages of red, yellow, and orange unsweetened powdered drink mix;

• paintbrushes;
• cups of water;
• glitter; and remember to bring your
• Coloring Creations Kit!

What to do:

Write children's names on their pages. Set out paintbrushes and the powdered drink mix.

1. Hand out the activity pages, and have children color their pictures except for the flames.

2. Give kids the water and paintbrushes. Have children paint the flames with water and then sprinkle small amounts of powdered drink mix on the wet area and watch as the water "dances" and looks like flames.

3. As children work, remind them that Shadrach, Meshach, and Abednego lived in a place where they weren't allowed to worship God. They were supposed to worship a silly statue instead. But, Shadrach, Meshach, and Abednego knew that God is the only real and true God, and they loved God so much that they worshipped him even though they knew they would get in trouble. Shadrach, Meshach, and Abednego stood up for their belief in God, and the king of the land had them punished.

4. Point to the picture of the "fourth man," and explain how God sent someone special to protect Shadrach, Meshach, and Abednego while they were in the fiery furnace. God saved Shadrach, Meshach, and Abednego because they weren't afraid to stand up for him.

5. Have children line the fourth man with glue and then sprinkle glitter on the man to show that he was sent from God. Encourage children to show their "Fiery Furnace" activity page to their families as a reminder that everyone should stand up for their belief in God.

Talk about:

Ask: • How do you think Shadrach, Meshach, and Abednego felt when they knew they would be thrown into the fire if they didn't bow down to the statue?

• Why do you think they were so brave and stood up for their belief in God?

• What is one way you can show you believe in God?

Say: Shadrach, Meshach, and Abednego loved God so much and knew that it was wrong to bow down to a statue. They knew they had to stand up for their belief in God.

Pray: Lord, help us to believe in you and not be afraid to tell others that we believe in you. In Jesus' name, amen.

"Stand firm in your faith. Be brave and strong for God"
(adapted from 1 Corinthians 16:13).

Daniel and the Lions

Daniel 6:1-23

What you need:

For each child...

- 1 copy of page 49
- 1 craft stick

You'll also need...

- dry Top Ramen noodles or curled gold gift ribbon, and remember to bring your
- Coloring Creations Kit!

What to do:

Write children's names on their pages.

1. Break up the Top Ramen noodles—or curl the gift ribbon—and give each child a handful. Cut a small slit in the space above Daniel's head on each page. Make slits large enough for children to slip a craft stick through. If you have older children who can use safety scissors, let them cut the slits.

2. Give each child an activity page and a craft stick. Explain that the kids are going to put curly manes on the lions and make the angel that kept Daniel safe in the lions' den. Give children some time to color their pages.

3. Have kids use glue sticks to spread glue on the lions' manes. Encourage children to gently press the noodles or ribbon into the glue. As children work, remind them that God sent an angel to be with Daniel and to shut the mouths of the lions so the lions couldn't hurt him.

4. When the pages are decorated, have kids use a marker to draw a smiley face on one end of a craft stick. Encourage kids to color the craft sticks white or gold to represent the angel's shining appearance.

5. Then, show children how to poke the craft stick through the slit from the back of the page, so that the angel's smiley face is showing above Daniel. Point out that God sent an angel to protect Daniel, and God will protect the kids, too. Encourage children to show the "Daniel and the Lions" activity page to their families as a reminder that God protects his people.

Talk about:

Ask: • How do you think Daniel felt when he was thrown into the pit with the lions?

• Have you ever been very afraid or scared of something? What was it?

• How did God protect Daniel?

• How does God protect you?

Say: God protects his people, just like God protected Daniel. That means you and me! Aren't you glad God is bigger and stronger than a room full of big, old scary lions? I am!

Pray: Lord, thank you that you take care of us. Keep us safe this week, just like you kept Daniel safe. We love you Jesus. In your name, amen.

"The angel of the Lord protects God's people"
(adapted from Psalm 34:7).

Permission to photocopy this coloring page from *Coloring Creations: 52 Bible Activity Pages* granted for local church use. Copyright © Group Publishing, Inc., P.O. Box 481, Loveland, CO 80539. www.grouppublishing.com

Jonah and the Big Fish

Jonah 1:1–3:10

What you need:

For each child...

- 1 copy of page 51
- fish crackers

You'll also need...

- blue cellophane, and remember to bring your
- Coloring Creations Kit!

What to do:

Write children's names on their pages. Set out the blue cellophane and the fish crackers.

1. Hand out the activity pages, and encourage children to color them.

2. Give kids several fish crackers, and have them glue the crackers onto the picture in the water around the big fish.

3. Finally, have kids tape a piece of blue cellophane over the entire picture to represent water. As children work, remind them that God had a special job for Jonah, but Jonah didn't want to do it. Jonah didn't obey God at first and tried to run away. God had a big fish swallow Jonah because Jonah had disobeyed. When Jonah told God he was sorry for disobeying, God had the big fish spit Jonah back out. After the fish spit Jonah onto the shore, Jonah obeyed God and did the special job that God wanted him to do.

Encourage children to show the "Jonah and the Big Fish" activity page to their families as a reminder that everyone should obey God.

Talk about:

Ask: • **Why do you think Jonah didn't want to obey God?**

• **Why should we obey God?**

Say: **Jonah didn't want to obey God at first. He tried to run away from God, but that didn't work! He ended up in the belly of a big fish! God was sad; he wanted Jonah to do what he asked him to do. God wanted Jonah to obey. God wants each of us to obey him. It makes God happy when we obey.**

Pray: **Lord, help us to obey you and do what you want us to do. In Jesus' name, amen.**

"This is love for God: to obey his commands"
(1 John 5:3a).

Foreign Visitors Worship Jesus

Matthew 2:1-12

What you need:

For each child...
- 1 copy of page 53
- 1 star sticker

You'll also need...
- Christmas tree tinsel,
- pieces of purple or red fabric,
- scented extract such as vanilla or almond, and remember to bring your
- Coloring Creations Kit!

What to do:

Write children's names on their pages. Use scissors to cut the Christmas tree tinsel into small pieces. Set out the tinsel, scraps of fabric, star stickers, and glue.

1. Give each child an activity page, and have kids use the crayons to color the page.

2. Show children the men in the picture, and explain that the men probably wore purple or red clothing, which was a sign of wealth and honor. Encourage kids to glue a piece of red or purple fabric to each of the men in the picture.

3. Encourage kids to put a star sticker in the sky above the men. Tell the kids that the foreign visitors heard about the birth of Jesus and the men wanted to find Jesus. God helped the men find Jesus by putting a star in the sky that helped to guide the men to Jesus.

4. Point out the foreign visitors' gifts. Explain that the men were so excited to see Jesus that they brought him wonderful and expensive gifts. One man brought gold. One man brought frankincense, and one man brought myrrh.

5. Encourage kids to glue a piece of tinsel onto one man's gift and to dab a few drops of extract onto the other two gifts. Explain that one way we can worship God is to give him gifts. Tell children that one gift they can give Jesus is to worship him and spend time with him. God wants everyone to worship Jesus and get to know Jesus. Encourage children to show the "Foreign Visitors Worship Jesus" activity page to their families as a reminder that everyone can worship Jesus.

Talk about:

Ask: • **How do you think the foreign visitors felt when they gave their gifts to Jesus?**

• **What gifts can you give Jesus?**

• **How can you give Jesus a gift of worship?**

Say: **Even though the men were from very far away and they'd never seen Jesus before, God still wanted them to worship Jesus and get to know Jesus. God wants everyone in the whole world to know Jesus.**

Pray: **Jesus, we love you. We want to give you gifts every day. We are so glad that everyone in the world can worship and get to know you. Thanks for being our God. In Jesus' name, amen.**

"Come, let us bow down in worship, let us kneel before the Lord our Maker"

(Psalm 95:6).

John Baptizes Jesus

Matthew 3:13-17

What you need:

For each child...

- 1 copy of page 55
- 8x8-inch square of blue paper
- small piece of sticky tack

You'll also need...

- white facial tissues, and remember to bring your
- Coloring Creations Kit!

What to do:

Write children's names on their pages.

1. Give each child an activity page. After children have colored their pictures, give each child an 8x8-inch square of blue paper. Tell kids they are going to create a curtain of water that can be pulled up and down over Jesus.

2. Have kids make half-inch accordion-type folds back and forth (as if making a fan) in the blue paper. Tape the lower edge of the blue paper to the bottom of the picture. Add a dot of sticky tack to the top edge of the curtain, and tack it to a spot just below Jesus and John—the sticky tack will hold the curtain of water down until children pull it up. Remind kids that Jesus wanted everyone to know he was God's Son. John the Baptist baptized Jesus in a river of water. Jesus went down into the water and came back up. Let children pull the "water" over Jesus.

3. Explain that the people who watched John baptize Jesus heard God say, "This is my Son." They saw God's Spirit come to Jesus like a dove. Encourage children to add a dove to their picture by tearing off a 2x3-inch piece of tissue, twisting it in the middle and then gluing the center of the tissue onto the top of their activity page.

Encourage children to show the "John Baptizes Jesus" activity page to their families as a reminder that Jesus is God's Son.

Talk about:

Ask: • Who is God's Son?

• What important things did God's Son do?

• How can you show that you believe in God's Son?

Say: Jesus wants everyone to know that he is God's Son. He came from heaven to show us how to be forgiven. Jesus took our sin and died in our place. When we pray, when we read our Bibles, when we go to church, and when we share Jesus' love with others, we show that we believe Jesus is God's Son.

Pray: Lord Jesus, we believe you are God's Son. Thank you for coming to be our Savior. In Jesus' name, amen.

"This is my Son, whom I love. Listen to him!"

(Mark 9:7b).

Jesus Wants Us to Follow Him

Matthew 4:18-25

What you need:

For each child...

- 1 copy of page 57

You'll also need...

- ink pads,
- glue brushes,
- glitter, and remember to bring your
- Coloring Creations Kits!

What to do:

Write children's names on their pages. Set out the ink pads, markers, glue, glue brushes, and glitter.

1. Give each child an activity page. Have children first color the page using washable markers.

2. Demonstrate to kids how to create footprints across their pages by making a fist, placing the bottom portion of the hand (where the pinkie is) on the ink pad, stamping it down onto the page, and then using their pinkie fingers to stamp the "toe prints" at the top of the foot. Help children with the first several prints, and then let them try it on their own.

3. Once students have stamped the "footprints" across their pages, set out dishes of glue and glue brushes. Encourage children to use the glue brushes to trace the footprints with glue. Help each child sprinkle some glitter onto the glue—this will make the footprints look extra special!

4. As children work, remind them that God wants everyone to follow Jesus. God sent us Jesus to show us the things we should do—like praying, helping people, and loving each other. Point out that the disciples in the picture were Jesus' special friends who followed Jesus everywhere and learned how to do the things he did. Remind children that Jesus wants us to be his special friends too. We can follow in Jesus' footsteps the same way the disciples did long ago.

Encourage children to show the "Jesus Wants Us to Follow Him" activity page to their families as a reminder that it is important to follow Jesus' example.

Talk about:

Ask: • **Who is someone that you like to copy? What things does this person do?**

• **What are some things Jesus did that you can do, too?**

• **Why is it important to follow Jesus?**

Say: **Jesus showed us how to pray to God, love each other, and help each other too. We can do those same things, just as Jesus did!**

Pray: **God, please help us to learn more about Jesus every day so we can do the things he did and follow him like you want us to. Thank you for Jesus and for showing us how to do things that make you happy. We love you, God! In Jesus' name, amen.**

"Follow in [Christ's] steps"
(1 Peter 2:21b).

God Hears Our Prayers

Matthew 6:5-14

What you need:

For each child...

• 1 copy of page 59

You'll also need...

• light colored construction paper, and remember to bring your
• Coloring Creations Kit!

What to do:

Write children's names on their pages. Before class cut out cartoon dialogue bubble shapes from light-colored construction paper. You will need one for each child in the class. Set the dialogue bubbles, crayons, and glue on the craft table for the children.

1. Show children the picture of the girl praying. Ask children to imagine what the girl might be talking to God about. Pass out the dialogue bubble shapes. Explain to children that in cartoons, artists use these dialogue bubbles to show what a character is thinking. The artists draw or write inside the bubble what the person is thinking.

2. Instruct children to draw a picture of something that they would like to talk to God about; remind kids that they can pray to God about anything at all. When children are finished, have them glue the dialogue bubble next to the girl's head on the picture.

3. Allow children to use crayons or markers to color the rest of the picture. As kids work, remind them that God hears their prayers when they pray. Encourage children to show the "God Hears Our Prayers" activity page to their families as a reminder that God hears everyone's prayers.

Talk about:

Ask: • **How do you feel knowing that God hears your prayers?**

• **If you could ask God anything what would it be?**

Say: **God loves to hear your prayers. You can talk to God about anything that's important to you. Let's take a moment and pray to God right now.**

Allow children to take turns making short sentence prayers to God about what they placed on their picture. Make sure each child has a turn to pray.

Pray: **God, we love you. Thank you for listening to our prayers. In Jesus' name, amen.**

"Listen to my prayer, O God"

(Psalm 55:1a).

God Is So Good

Matthew 6:25-34

What you need:

For each child...

- 1 copy of page 61
- scraps of fabric
- stickers
- dry cereal or rice

You'll also need...

- your Coloring Creations Kit!

What to do:

Write children's names on their pages. Set out the crayons, glue, fabric scraps, and dry cereal or rice.

1. Give each child an activity page. Have children first color the picture using the crayons. Read verse 1 from Psalm 136 to the kids, and ask them to share a way that God has been good to them and has taken care of them. Point out that the people in the picture are praying. Praying is one way we can thank God for all he gives to us.

2. Have children glue fabric scraps onto the people in the picture as a reminder to be thankful for their clothes, and then have them glue the dry cereal onto the table in the picture as a reminder to be thankful for the food God gives them.

3. Give students stickers or other objects they may be thankful for, such as animals, flowers, or people. Have kids put the stickers on the picture. Encourage children to show the "God Is So Good" activity page to their families as a reminder to thank God for all the many blessings in life.

Talk about:

Ask: • What things are you thankful for that God has given to you?

• How can you show God that you are thankful for those things?

Say: God loves us so very much! God wants to fill our lives with things that make us happy. It is important that we thank God for being so good by doing things that make God happy too, such as loving him and loving all the people around us.

Pray: God, thank you for being so good to us. Thanks for giving us everything we need and everything we love. We love you, God! In Jesus' name, amen.

"Give thanks to the Lord, for he is good"
(Psalm 136:1a).

Permission to photocopy this coloring page from *Coloring Creations: 52 Bible Activity Pages* granted for local church use. Copyright © Group Publishing, Inc., P.O. Box 481, Loveland, CO 80539. www.grouppublishing.com

Jesus Feeds a Hungry Crowd

Matthew 14:13-21

What you need:

For each child...

• 1 copy of page 63
• about 10 to 15 sequins
• 2 small brown construction paper rectangles

You'll also need...

• your Coloring Creations Kit!

What to do:

Write children's names on their pages. Cut two small bread-shaped rectangles the same size as the loaves of bread on the activity page.

1. Give each child an activity page, and encourage kids to begin coloring the pages. Read the Bible story (from Matthew 14) to children, and point out all the food that God provided for the people in the story.

2. Give each child several sequins and small pieces of brown paper. Explain that the sequins are fish scales, and the pieces of brown paper are loaves of bread. Help children place dots of glue all over the page, among the crowd of people.

3. Encourage children to place a sequin "fish" or a paper "loaf" onto each of the dots. Point out how much food there is—enough for everyone in the crowd! As children work, remind them that Jesus will provide for them, just as he provided for all the people in the crowd that day. Encourage children to show the "Jesus Feeds a Hungry Crowd" activity page to their families as a reminder that Jesus takes care of and provides for his people.

Talk about:

Ask: • **How did Jesus show that he cared about the hungry people?**

• **How do you think the people felt when they saw this miracle?**

• **What has God provided for you that makes you happy?**

Say: Jesus showed that he cared for all the people by providing food for their hungry tummies. That made the people happy. When God provides food, nice warm blankets for us to sleep on, or a mom and dad to take care of us, that should make us happy also.

Pray: Dear Lord, please take care of me just as you took care of all the hungry people in that crowd. Thank you, Jesus. I love you. In Jesus' name, amen.

"[God] richly provides us with everything for our enjoyment"
(1 Timothy 6:17b).

Jesus Walks on Water

Matthew 14:22-33

What you need:

For each child...

- 1 copy of page 65
- 5 strands of blue curly ribbon (about 3 inches long)
- 1 fabric scrap about the size of the sail on the picture

You'll also need...

- your Coloring Creations Kit!

What to do:

Write children's names on their pages. Cut five pieces of blue curly ribbon about three inches long and a fabric scrap about the same size as the sail on the activity page for each child.

1. Give each child an activity page. Encourage children to begin coloring the page. Read the Bible verse to children, and point out the fear on the disciples' faces. Explain to children that the disciples had been fishing in the boat when a big, scary storm came up. Point to Jesus walking on the water with his arm reaching out to the disciples in the boat. Tell kids that when the disciples saw Jesus walking on the water, it really scared them! They'd never seen anything like it—people aren't supposed to walk on water. Then, Peter tried walking on the water too. Peter was afraid at first, but then he trusted Jesus and had faith in him. When Peter had faith in Jesus, he was able to walk on the water.

2. Have kids draw themselves walking on the water next to Peter, remind kids that they can have faith in Jesus, just as Peter did.

3. Show children how to carefully place a line of glue on one side of the sail and in the arch of the stormy wave. Have kids press one end of their piece of fabric into the line of glue on the sail and one end of their ribbon into the glue on the wave.

4. Encourage kids to blow on the paper and watch as the ribbon and the fabric wave in the wind! Encourage children to show the "Jesus Walks on Water" activity page to their families as a reminder that everyone can have faith in Jesus.

Talk about:

Ask: • How did Peter show his faith in Jesus?

• How can you show your faith in Jesus?

Say: Jesus can help us have faith in him. Just as Peter had faith that Jesus would keep him safe on the water, we can trust Jesus to help us and care for us.

Pray: Dear Lord, help me to have faith in you and not be afraid. In Jesus' name, amen.

"But Jesus immediately said to them: 'Take courage! It is I. Don't be afraid' "

(Matthew 14:27).

Jesus Heals the Sick

Mark 1:29–2:12

What you need:

For each child...

- 1 copy of page 67
- plastic adhesive bandage
- cotton ball
- cotton swab
- strip of gauze
- licorice ropes

You'll also need...

- your Coloring Creations Kit!

What to do:

Write children's names on their pages. Set out the glue, plastic adhesive bandages, cotton balls, cotton swabs, and gauze strips.

1. Give each child an activity page. Have children first color the picture using the crayons. Explain to children that Jesus healed all different kinds of diseases, and people came from everywhere to be healed by him.

2. Have children glue the first aid supplies all over their picture as a reminder that Jesus healed the people that came to him.

3. Encourage kids to glue the licorice ropes onto the ropes in the picture to show how the paralyzed man's friends lowered him to Jesus to be healed.

4. Finally, have children glue a strip of gauze over the paralyzed man as a blanket. Encourage children to show the "Jesus Heals the Sick" activity page to their families as a reminder of the many ways Jesus healed people.

Talk about:

Ask:
- **Have you ever been sick? What did it feel like?**
- **How did it feel when you got better?**
- **How do you think the sick people felt when Jesus healed them?**
- **Who is someone you can pray for God to help feel better?**

Say: Jesus cares about the way we feel. When we're sick and feel yucky, Jesus wants to help us feel better. When Jesus lived on earth, he healed many people who were sick. We can also pray and ask God to heal people we know who are sick.

Pray: God, thank you for healing us when we are sick and for taking such good care of our friends and family members who are sick. We know that you love us and help us feel better. We love you, God! In Jesus' name, amen.

"And Jesus healed many who had various diseases"
(Mark 1:34a).

Jesus Calms the Storm

Mark 4:35-41

What you need:

For each child...
- 1 copy of page 69
- cotton balls

You'll also need...
- white crayons,
- blue tempera paint,
- water,
- small paintbrushes,
- blue powdered gelatin mix (optional), and remember to bring your
- Coloring Creations Kit!

What to do:

Write children's names on their pages. Dilute the blue tempera paint with water to make a wash that will allow the color to show through on the page. Use a white crayon to draw a cross on the sail of each page; be sure to press hard and go over the lines a few times so the lines are solid.

1. Distribute the activity pages, and have kids color their picture—except for the sail. Tell kids that they should hurry to color the people in the boat because a storm is coming! Explain to children that when a storm came up and rocked the boat, Jesus' followers were scared and thought they were going to die. The disciples forgot one important thing—Jesus was with them! Even though the wind and waves battered the boat, Jesus protected them.

2. Bring out the paint wash and paintbrushes, and have kids paint the wash over the entire picture. Encourage children to make the pictures look like a stormy, scary sea. As kids paint over it, the white cross will appear on the sail. Point out the cross, and explain that it represents Jesus because he died on the cross for them. Jesus was always there with the people in the boat, and he was taking care of them!

3. When the paint is dry, have children glue several cotton balls onto the clouds in the picture.

4. For extra dazzle, "draw" a few lines of glue in the waves of the sea, and have kids sprinkle some blue powdered gelatin mix on the glue. As the powder soaks into the glue, it will darken into a "stormy" blue color—it will sparkle and smell good, too!

Encourage children to take the "Jesus Calms the Storm" activity page home as a reminder that Jesus is always there to help during scary times.

Talk about:

Ask: • What things scare you?

• How did Jesus help his friends during the storm?

• How can Jesus help you when you're scared?

Say: Jesus is so powerful he made the wind and sea obey him! Jesus' friends learned that they could trust Jesus to take care of them. It's great to know that Jesus will take care of us, especially when we're scared.

Pray: Thank you, Jesus, for taking care of us. Help us to trust you when we're scared. In your name, amen.

"**Don't be afraid; just believe**"
(Luke 8:50a).

Jesus Loves Kids

Mark 10:13-16

What you need:

For each child...
- 1 copy of page 71
- two ½x2-inch brown felt ovals

You'll also need...
- your Coloring Creations Kit!

What to do:

Write children's names on their pages. Cut out two brown felt ovals for each child.

1. Give each of the children an activity page. Read the Bible verse to the children. Point out that, in the picture, Jesus has his arms around the children. The children are happy and safe in Jesus' arms.

2. Explain that the kids will draw a picture of themselves next to Jesus and the other children in the picture. Then they will glue the brown felt pieces onto Jesus' arms so that he can hug the children. Provide crayons or markers, glue, and the felt ovals. Allow children ample time to color their activity pages and to draw themselves next to Jesus and the other children.

3. When the kids are finished, show them how to glue the felt oval-arms on the picture to look like the arms are wrapped around the children. As kids work, remind them that Jesus loves them, too. Encourage children to show the "Jesus Loves Kids" activity page to their families as a reminder that Jesus loves kids.

Talk about:

Ask: • What do you think the children might have thought about Jesus?

• How can you use your hands to show others that Jesus loves them?

• What do you think Jesus would say to you if you were on his lap?

Say: Jesus was kind to children. Our Bible verse says that Jesus put his loving hands on the children and blessed them. That means Jesus made the children happy when he touched them. He used his kind hands to make them happy. When we choose to use kind hands to love and help others, we make them happy too.

Pray: Dear Lord, help me to have kind and loving hands like Jesus, so I can bless my friends the way that Jesus blessed children. In Jesus' name, amen.

"And [Jesus] took the children in his arms, put his hands on them and blessed them"

(Mark 10:16).

Crowds Welcome Jesus to Jerusalem

Mark 11:1-11

What you need:

For each child...
- 1 copy of page 73
- crisp rice cereal
- 2-inch fabric squares (1 or 2 per child)

You'll also need...
- ½ teaspoon measuring spoon,
- water,
- green construction paper, and remember to bring your
- Coloring Creations Kit!

What to do:

Write children's names on their pages. Cut out one or two green palm leaves for each child.

1. Give each child an activity page. Encourage children to color their pages. Ask children to tell you why it's hard to be quiet when other kids are celebrating. Tell children Jesus' friends were celebrating, and some other people told Jesus' friends to quiet down. Read the Bible verse, and explain that this celebration for Jesus was so special that no one could keep quiet.

2. Have children spread glue on the road in front of Jesus. Instruct kids to press one or two fabric square coats and their palm leaves into the glue.

3. Then encourage kids to sprinkle a small handful of crisp rice cereal over the glue still showing. Sprinkle a half tea-spoonful of water over the glued rice on each paper. As the rice begins to crackle, tell children that Jesus said if his friends kept quiet, the rocks would cry out. Palm Sunday was so important that people couldn't keep quiet. The people in the picture can't speak now but the rocks can.

4. Have kids carefully bend over their paper and listen to the sounds of the rocks on their pictures. Jesus is so special that no one can keep quiet about him!

Encourage children to show the "Crowds Welcome Jesus to Jerusalem" activity page to their families as a reminder that everyone can celebrate Jesus!

Talk about:

Ask: • **What do you think the people said to tell Jesus they were happy to see him?**

• **What words can we use to celebrate Jesus?**

Say: **Let's pick one thing to say together so we can celebrate Jesus too.** Have the kids hold up their papers and shout together several words of celebration.

Pray: **Jesus, we are so glad you came, and we want to celebrate like the people in our picture did. We are too happy to keep quiet about you! In your name, amen.**

" 'I tell you,' he replied, 'if they keep quiet,
the stones will cry out' "
(Luke 19:40).

The Empty Tomb

Mark 16:1-8

What you need:

For each child...

- 1 copy of page 75
- 1 craft stick

You'll also need...

- brown construction paper or fun foam, and remember to bring your
- Coloring Creations Kit!

What to do:

Write children's names on their pages. Cut a horizontal slit along the floor of the tomb on each activity page; make the slit the length of the tomb and a few inches to each side. The children will be moving a craft stick, with the stone attached, back and forth to cover and uncover the tomb opening.

1. Give each child an activity page and a piece of brown construction paper or fun foam. Encourage kids to color the page. Point out the two women standing next to the tomb. Remind the children that the women came to take care of Jesus' body, but the tomb was empty! The women couldn't find Jesus' body anywhere because Jesus is alive!

2. Help children draw and cut out a circle on the brown paper or fun foam that's big enough to cover the tomb opening.

3. When children have finished their stones, have them each glue the stone to the end of a craft stick and then insert the craft stick inside the slit in front of the tomb. Demonstrate how the stone can be rolled away to reveal an empty tomb. Encourage children to show the "Empty Tomb" activity page to their families and show how the rolling stone reveals an empty tomb because Jesus is alive!

Talk about:

Ask: • What do you think the women thought when they saw the stone rolled away from Jesus' tomb?

• Why do you think the tomb was empty?

Say: We know Jesus is God's Son. The women couldn't see Jesus' body because he wasn't there. Jesus is alive!

Pray: Dear God, thank you for sending your Son, Jesus, to die for us. Help us to remember that he is not in a tomb, but he is alive! In Jesus' name, amen.

"He has risen!"

(Luke 24:6a).

Mary and Joseph Travel to Bethlehem

Luke 2:1-5

What you need:

For each child...
- 1 copy of page 77
- 1 sugar cube

You'll also need...
- sandpaper, and remember to bring your
- Coloring Creations Kit!

What to do:

Write children's names on their pages. Set out the sugar cubes, glue, and crayons. Cut the sandpaper into strips that will fit on the illustration of the road.

1. Instruct children to color Mary, Joseph, and the donkey as you talk. Tell the story of how Mary and Joseph had to travel to Jerusalem (found in Luke 2). Explain that God had a special plan for Jesus—Mary's baby. God had a plan for Jesus to be born in Jerusalem. The only problem was that Jesus' family lived very far away from Jerusalem!

2. Show children the donkey in the picture, and tell children how God used the donkey to help Mary and Joseph get to Bethlehem. The donkey helped carry Jesus' family from their hometown to Jerusalem. Encourage children to glue a sugar cube in Joseph's hand near the donkey's mouth to thank the donkey for being a part of God's special plan.

3. Have children glue the sandpaper on the road as a reminder that God planned a path for Mary, Joseph, and the donkey to take. Remind kids that they can know that God has a special plan for each one of them. Encourage kids to show the "Mary and Joseph Travel to Bethlehem" activity page to their families as a reminder that God has special plans for everyone.

Talk about:

Ask:
- **What special plans did God have for Jesus?**
- **How did the donkey help make those plans happen?**
- **What kinds of plans do you think God has for you?**

Say: God had big plans for Jesus. He has plans for each and every one of you, too.

Pray: God, we thank you for having an important plan for every one of us. Help us obey you and your plans. In Jesus' name, amen.

" 'For I know the plans I have for you,'
declares the Lord"
(Jeremiah 29:11a).

Jesus Is Born For Us!

Luke 2:1-20

What you need:

For each child...
- 1 copy of page 79
- pieces of fabric

You'll also need...
- glitter glue, and remember to bring your
- Coloring Creations Kit!

What to do:

Write children's names on their pages. Cut pieces of fabric a little bigger than baby Jesus so that the children can wrinkle the fabric slightly and it will still fit over him (about 1½x2-inches).

1. Give each of the children an activity page, and have them begin to color it. As children work, read the Bible story (from Luke 2) to them. Point out that baby Jesus is wrapped in a blanket, and his parents are taking care of him.

2. Have children glue the piece of fabric over the baby Jesus in the picture. Tell children that God gave us parents to take care of us, just as Jesus' parents are taking care of him. And God gave Jesus to all of us so that Jesus could help us get closer to God. God had a special plan for Jesus to die on the cross and forgive us of our sins. Jesus didn't stay dead, though; he came alive again and now lives in heaven with God. Jesus is the way to God, and when we believe in him, we will have life forever with him in heaven.

3. Encourage kids to use glitter glue to each make a cross in the sky above the manger. Set the pages aside to dry until the children are ready to go home. Encourage children to show the "Jesus Is Born for Us!" activity page to their families as a reminder that Jesus was born for us.

Talk about:

Ask:
- **Why do you think God gave baby Jesus to Mary and Joseph?**
- **How did Mary and Joseph take care of baby Jesus?**
- **Why do you think God gave baby Jesus to us?**
- **How has Jesus taken care of you?**

Say: God saw that Mary and Joseph would be the perfect parents for baby Jesus. Mary and Joseph loved God and wanted to teach their children to love God also. God gave baby Jesus to us so that Jesus would live a perfect life and die for all the bad things we do. When we believe God sent Jesus to be born and to forgive our sins, we will have life forever with Jesus in heaven.

Pray: Dear Lord, thank you for sending your Son, Jesus, to be born for us so we can have life with you forever. In Jesus' name, amen.

"Jesus is the way to God"
(adapted from John 14:6).

Permission to photocopy this coloring page from *Coloring Creations: 52 Bible Activity Pages* granted for local church use. Copyright © Group Publishing, Inc., P.O. Box 481, Loveland, CO 80539. www.grouppublishing.com

Young Jesus Teaches in the Synagogue

Luke 2:39-52

What you need:

For each child...
- 1 copy of page 81

You'll also need...
- colored chalk,
- non-aerosol hair spray,
- age-appropriate magazines, and remember to bring your
- Coloring Creations Kit!

What to do:

Write children's names on their pages. Set out the magazines and the colored chalk.

1. Have children color their pictures with the colored chalk. Tell kids teachers use chalk to write on chalkboards and teach their students.

2. When kids are finished coloring, spray their pictures with the hair spray so that the chalk won't smear. Wait a few minutes for the hair spray to dry. Explain that when Jesus was a little boy, he went to the synagogue and taught a group of men about the Bible and about God.

3. Have children look through the magazines and cut out pictures of people teaching others. Kids could also look for things that remind them of school such as a book, a backpack, a sack lunch, or a teacher.

4. Have children glue the pictures around the edges and on the back of the "Young Jesus Teaches in the Synagogue" activity page. Remind kids that, as Jesus grew, he got smarter and smarter. God will help them learn new things and get smarter as they grow up too!

5. Help children roll their papers into scrolls, and explain that a scroll is what Jesus would have used to teach the men about God. Encourage children to unroll their scrolls and use the "Young Jesus Teaches in the Synagogue" activity page to "teach" their families that God can help them grow wise and learn new things.

Talk about:

Ask: • What do you think Jesus was teaching about?

• What is one thing you know about Jesus that you could teach to someone else?

Say: Every day Jesus learned new things. He had to learn how to crawl, walk, run, read, and share—just as you have done. Every day Jesus grew smarter and stronger, and every day you are growing smarter and stronger. You are not babies anymore; you are growing into big boys and girls. God is helping you to grow bigger and smarter every day.

Pray: Lord, thank you for helping us to grow every day. Help us to always be wise. In Jesus' name, amen.

"And Jesus grew in wisdom and stature, and in favor with God and men"
(Luke 2:52).

Jesus Gives the Disciples an Amazing Catch

Luke 5:1-11

What you need:

For each child...

- 1 copy of page 83
- 2x4-inch piece of hairnet (plastic mesh from a bag of oranges or onions can be used as an alternative)

You'll also need...

- an ink pad, and remember to bring your
- Coloring Creations Kit!

What to do:

Write children's names on their pages. Cut a hairnet or plastic mesh into 2x4-inch pieces. You will need one piece for each child. Set out the hairnets and an ink pad.

1. Give each child an activity page. As children color the page, remind them that Jesus filled the disciples' nets with fish to help them learn that they must be fishers of men. Have children point to the fish and count them. Explain that there are many, many people who need to hear about Jesus and that God wants us to be fishers of men. Help kids understand that we "catch" people for God by sharing his love with others.

2. Have children add scales to the fish by each pressing a finger onto the ink pad and then adding a fingerprint to a fish. As kids touch each fish, have them name a specific person with whom they can share Jesus' love.

3. Have each child glue the hairnet or plastic mesh onto the catch of fish. Encourage the children to show the "Jesus Gives the Disciples an Amazing Catch" activity page to their families as a reminder to share Jesus' love with others.

Talk about:

Ask:
- What does it mean to be a fisher of men?
- Who can you tell about Jesus?

Say: When we tell others about Jesus, we are being fishers of men. It makes God happy when we are his fishermen and share Jesus' love with others.

Pray: Lord, help us be fishers of men and share Jesus' love with everyone we know. In Jesus' name, amen.

" 'Come, follow me,' Jesus said, 'and I will make you fishers of men' "

(Matthew 4:19).

Permission to photocopy this coloring page from *Coloring Creations: 52 Bible Activity Pages* granted for local church use. Copyright © Group Publishing, Inc., P.O. Box 481, Loveland, CO 80539. www.grouppublishing.com

Jesus Gives the Disciples an Amazing Catch

The Good Samaritan

Luke 10:25-37

What you need:

For each child...

- 1 copy of page 85
- small piece of fabric or colored construction paper

You'll also need...

- age-appropriate magazines, and remember to bring your
- Coloring Creations Kit!

What to do:

Write children's names on their pages. Cut a small piece of fabric or construction paper approximately two inches wide by three inches long for each child.

1. Hand out the activity pages, and encourage kids to begin coloring. Point out the hurt man, and remind children the man had been robbed and beaten. He was hurt and couldn't walk. People came by who could have helped the man, but they pretended they didn't see him and walked away. Then a man who was his enemy walked past, but this man stopped and helped him.

2. Explain that children are going to help the hurt man by giving the man a blanket. Help children glue the piece of material over the hurt man. Ask children what other things they could do to help the hurt man.

3. Encourage kids to look through a magazine to find things to help the man, and have them tear or cut out the pictures and glue the pictures onto their activity page. As children work, remind them that God loves us, and he wants us to love others and care for them, just as the Samaritan man helped the hurt man. Encourage children to show the "The Good Samaritan" activity page to their families as a reminder to help others.

Talk about:

Ask: • How do you think the hurt man felt when someone finally helped him?

• Have you ever helped someone who you really didn't like very much? What did you do?

• What are some ways you can be a good Samaritan and help someone else?

Say: We know Jesus wants us to help people because he tells us so in the Bible. When we help others, we are sharing God's love.

Pray: Lord, show us ways we can help other people so they will know that you love them. In Jesus' name, amen.

"Love your enemies and do good to them"
(adapted from Luke 6:35).

Jesus Changes Water Into Wine

John 2:1-11

What you need:

For each child...

- 1 copy of page 87

You'll also need...

- grape Kool-Aid crystals,
- shallow bowls,
- Bible,
- water,
- sponges, and remember to bring your
- Coloring Creations Kit!

What to do:

Write children's names on their pages. Pour the grape Kool-Aid crystals into half of the bowls and pour water into the other half. Cut several sponges into two-inch squares, and set them on the table.

1. Give each child an activity page. Open your Bible to John 2, and tell the story of Jesus at the wedding; stop reading at the point in the story when the servants bring out the jars of water. Instruct children to rub glue on the mouths of the jars. Then have kids sprinkle the grape Kool-Aid crystals on the glue and secure the crystals in place with their thumbs.

2. Continue telling the story up until the point where Jesus changes the water into wine. Have kids dampen their sponges in the water and then blot the sponges on the mouth of the jar. The blue crystals will turn purple! Remind kids that Jesus changed the blue water into yummy purple wine.

3. Have kids finish coloring their activity pages. Encourage children to take their "Jesus Changes Water Into Wine" activity page home, and use it to explain to someone else how Jesus helped his friends at the wedding.

Talk about:

Ask: • How do you think Jesus' friends felt when they saw Jesus perform the miracle?

• How does Jesus help you?

• What can you do the next time you need help?

Say: Jesus loves to help us. We can ask Jesus for help by praying to him and telling him what we need.

Pray: Jesus, thank you for loving us and helping us. Please help us be helpful to our friends and family, just as you were helpful to your friends at the wedding. In Jesus' name, amen.

"The Lord is my helper; I will not be afraid"

(Hebrews 13:6a).

The Woman at the Well

John 4:5-42

What you need:

For each child...

• 1 copy of page 89
• one 3-inch length of string or yarn

You'll also need...

• card stock,
• hole punch, and remember to bring your
• Coloring Creations Kit!

What to do:

Write children's names on their pages. Cut a bucket shape (about one to two inches) from card stock; you will need one for each child. Cut a horizontal slit in the top of the well in each activity page. Make the slit wide enough for the paper bucket to fit through.

1. Give each child an activity page. Encourage children to begin coloring their pages. Tell children that the woman in the picture gave Jesus some water because Jesus was thirsty. The water that the woman gave Jesus was just regular water, like we might drink out of a faucet. After we drink some water, we'll probably get thirsty again, but Jesus told the woman that whoever drinks the water he gives would never be thirsty again.

2. Give each child a paper bucket. Tell children to think about some special things we get from Jesus and to draw one special thing on the bucket.

3. Help children each punch a hole in their bucket and then tie the string or yarn through the hole. Tape the other end of the string to the back of the activity page so children can move the bucket up and down in the well. Encourage kids to show the "Woman at the Well" activity page to their families as a reminder that Jesus' love is forever.

Talk about:

Ask: • **What kind of water do you think Jesus was talking about?**

• **What are some things Jesus gives us?**

Say: **We know that food or water only make us less hungry or thirsty for a little while, and then we get hungry or thirsty again. Things that make us happy can break or get lost or wear out. But what we get from Jesus will last forever.**

Pray: **Dear God, thank you for loving us and sending Jesus to us. We know that Jesus' love will always be more than enough for us. In Jesus' name, amen.**

"But whoever drinks the water I give him will never thirst"

(John 4:14a).

Jesus Is the Good Shepherd

John 10:1-18

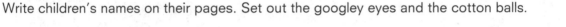

What you need:

For each child...
- 1 copy of page 91
- 1 heart bead or heart sticker
- googley eyes
- cotton balls
- 1 chenille wire

You'll also need...
- your Coloring Creations Kit!

What to do:

Write children's names on their pages. Set out the googley eyes and the cotton balls.

1. Give each child an activity page, a heart bead or heart sticker, and one chenille wire. Encourage children to begin coloring the page. As children work, remind them Jesus promised he would be our shepherd. Explain that a shepherd is a person who leads his or her sheep. The shepherd leads the sheep to food and water, to dry places when it is raining, and to safe places where the sheep can sleep at night. The shepherd loves the sheep and takes good care of the sheep. The sheep know the shepherd's voice, and they follow the shepherd wherever the shepherd leads.

2. Have children glue cotton balls and googley eyes onto the sheep and the chenille wire onto Jesus' staff. Read the Bible verse to the children, and explain that Jesus promised us he would guide us and take care of us. Jesus loves us, just as a shepherd loves the sheep. We can trust Jesus to protect us and to be there for us because he is our good shepherd.

3. Have children glue the heart bead or heart sticker on Jesus as a reminder that Jesus loves them even more than a shepherd loves the sheep. Encourage children to show the "Jesus Is the Good Shepherd" activity page to their families as a reminder that Jesus is the good shepherd, and he guides and protects his people.

Talk about:

Ask: • How can you follow Jesus, as the sheep follow their shepherd?

• How do you know that Jesus loves you?

Say: We can trust Jesus and follow the things he tells us to do such as being nice to our friends, obeying our parents, praying, and sharing Jesus' love with others. A shepherd always protects the sheep. A shepherd loves the sheep so much that the shepherd would even give his or her life for the sheep. Jesus gave his life for us when he died on the cross. Jesus loves us so much that he died to forgive our sins! Jesus is our good shepherd, and we can trust his love for us.

Pray: Jesus, thank you so much for your love. We are so glad that you are our good shepherd. Help us to trust you and to follow you, as sheep follow their shepherd. In your name, amen.

"The Lord is my shepherd"

(Psalm 23:1a).

Jesus Washes the Disciples' Feet

John 13:1-7

What you need:

For each child...

• 1 copy of page 93

You'll also need...

• watercolor paints,
• paintbrushes,
• cups of water,
• 1 washcloth per 9 or 10 children, and remember to bring your
• Coloring Creations Kit!

What to do:

Write children's names on their pages. Cut a washcloth into several small pieces. You will need enough pieces for each child to have one. Set out the watercolor paints and paintbrushes.

1. Give each child a piece of washcloth. Help kids glue the washcloth to Jesus' hands.

2. Encourage kids to use the watercolor paints to paint the picture. Explain that kids are using watercolors to paint their pictures as a reminder that Jesus used water to wash the disciples' feet.

3. As children work, remind them that Jesus was a good example of a servant. Explain that Jesus was serving his friends by washing their feet. Encourage children to show the "Jesus Washes the Disciples' Feet" activity page to their families as a reminder that everyone should serve others.

Talk about:

Ask: • **How do you think Jesus' disciples felt when Jesus served them and washed their feet?**

• **How do you think Jesus felt when he was serving his friends by washing their feet?**

• **What is one way that you have served your friends? How did that make you feel?**

Say: Jesus loved his disciples very much, and he wanted to show his disciples how much he loved them by doing something for them. Jesus washed his disciples' dirty feet! Jesus loved to serve others. It's good to be like Jesus and serve others. We can do things for other people to show them how much we love them. When we act like Jesus and serve others it makes him happy.

Pray: Dear Jesus, thank you for showing us how to be a good servant. Help us to serve others. In your name, amen.

"When I washed your feet, I set an example for you to follow. Do as I have done for you"
(adapted from John 13:14-15).

You Can Have a Friendship With Jesus

John 14:5-14

What you need:

For each child...

- 1 copy of page 95
- 1 heart bead

You'll also need...

- yarn,
- pen or pencil, and remember to bring your
- Coloring Creations Kit!

What to do:

Write children's names on their pages.

1. Give each child an activity page. While children color their pictures, provide a time for them to get to know one another better. Let children tell the group about their favorite food or game, how many brothers or sisters they have, or what kinds of pets they have. Tell kids that spending time together and learning new things about one another is how people get to know their friends better. Remind kids that they can get to know Jesus in the same ways—by spending time with him, going to church, praying, and learning the things in the Bible.

2. When children have finished coloring, help them use a pen or pencil to poke a small hole in the picture of the girl and another in Jesus.

3. Help children lace the heart bead onto the yarn and string the yarn through the holes. Tie the yarn behind the picture.

4. Let children move the heart from Jesus to the picture of the child as you remind them that Jesus shares his love with us and we can share our love with him. Let children move the heart back to Jesus and give ideas of how they can have a friendship with Jesus.

Encourage children to show the "You Can Have a Friendship With Jesus" activity page to their families and share with them how to get to know Jesus better.

Talk about:

Ask: • **How did it feel to get to know each other better?**

• **What can we do to get to know Jesus better?**

Say: **We begin a personal relationship with Jesus when we understand that he loves us and wants us to love him back. Jesus has shown his great love for us by dying for our sin. When we believe Jesus died for us and ask for his forgiveness, we are telling Jesus that we want to know him as our Savior and friend.**

Pray: **Lord, thank you for being my Savior and my friend. Help me to get to know you better and better every day. In Jesus' name, amen.**

"I want to know Christ"
(Philippians 3:10a).

God's Holy Spirit Is Like the Wind

Acts 2:1-21; 3:12-19

What you need:

For each child...
• 1 copy of page 97

You'll also need...
• white crayons,
• watercolor paints,
• water,
• water dishes,
• paintbrushes, and remember to bring your
• Coloring Creations Kit!

What to do:

Write children's names on their pages. Set out the watercolor paints, water dishes, and paintbrushes.

1. Give each child an activity page. Have children first color the swirling lines in the picture with white crayon. Explain to children that Jesus gave the Holy Spirit to us to be our helper. The Holy Spirit is God's way of being with us to help us make right choices and to know the things that God wants us to do or say. The Holy Spirit is always with us, even though we can't see him—just as we can't see the white crayon on our pages, even though we know it's there!

2. Have children color the page by painting all over it with the watercolor paints. Have kids observe that the paint won't cover up the swirling lines of crayon. Remind children that even though we can't see God's Holy Spirit, we can know he is like the wind or the white crayon—he is there even though we can't see him. Encourage children to show the "God's Holy Spirit Is Like the Wind" activity page to their families as a reminder that God's Holy Spirit is always with us even when we can't see him.

Talk about:

Ask: • Have you ever been outside and seen leaves blowing in the trees or on the ground? What makes them move? How do you know?

• When you need help making a right choice to do something, who can you ask for help?

• How does it make you feel to know that God's Holy Spirit is always with you even though you can't see him?

Say: Jesus gave us the Holy Spirit to always be with us and help us make right choices and know what to do. Even though we can't see God's Holy Spirit, we can know that the Holy Spirit is there by the things he does—just as we can know the wind is there by the things it does.

Pray: God, thank you for caring about us so much that you gave us your Holy Spirit to be with us always. We are so happy to know that we are never alone and that your Holy Spirit will help us make right choices. We love you, God! In Jesus' name, amen.

"The Holy Spirit will teach you"
(adapted from John 14:26).

Church Brings Us All Together

Acts 2:42-47

What you need:

For each child...
• 1 copy of page 99

You'll also need...
• yarn,
• glue brushes,
• glitter glue, and remember to bring your
• Coloring Creations Kit!

What to do:

Write children's names on their pages. Cut up five lengths of yarn per child. Set out the crayons, glue, glue brushes, and glitter glue.

1. Give each child an activity page. Have children first color the page using crayons. As kids work, explain to them that church is a place that brings everybody together with God. People come to church to love each other and to love God together.

2. Show children how to make a small cross with glitter glue at the top of their pages.

3. Give each child five lengths of yarn. Have children use the glue brushes to make lines of glue connecting the children to each other and to the cross. Then have kids press the yarn lengths onto the glue lines. As children work, remind them that church is a place that brings us all together with God. Encourage children to show the "Church Brings Us All Together" activity pages to their families as a reminder that church is a place of love and connection with people and with God.

Talk about:

Ask: • What is your favorite part of going to church? Why?

• How can you show love to your friends at church?

• What are some ways you and your friends at church together show God that you love him?

Say: Church is a place where everybody can come and learn more about God. We come here to worship God, showing God we love him. We can look forward to coming to church to see our friends and to worship God together!

Pray: God, thank you so much for bringing us all together to worship you. Help us to show your love to new people at church every time we come. We love you, God! In Jesus' name, amen.

"Let us go to the house of the Lord"
(Psalm 122:1b).

Permission to photocopy this coloring page from *Coloring Creations: 52 Bible Activity Pages* granted for local church use. Copyright © Group Publishing, Inc., P.O. Box 481, Loveland, CO 80539. www.grouppublishing.com

Paul and Silas Teach the Jailer That Everyone Can Know Jesus

Acts 16:16-34

What you need:

For each child...

- 1 copy of page 101
- small pieces of foil
- felt scraps

You'll also need...

- heart stickers, or a heart stamp and ink pad;
- toothpicks; and remember to bring your
- Coloring Creations Kit!

What to do:

Write children's names on their pages. Set out the crayons, heart stickers (or a heart stamp and ink pad), toothpicks, and glue.

1. Give each child an activity page. Have children first color the picture of Paul and Silas in prison. As kids color, explain to them that Paul and Silas told the jailer about Jesus. Paul and Silas helped the jailer understand that God loves all people—no matter what they look like, or where they live, or what language they speak. God wants everyone in the world to know Jesus.

2. Have children place a heart sticker (or a heart stamp) on each person in the picture to show that God loves each of the people.

3. Then have children glue toothpicks onto the bars of the prison, small pieces of foil to the jailer's armor, and some small scraps of felt onto Paul's and Silas' outfits. Remind children that they can also help other people know and love Jesus, just as Paul and Silas helped the jailer. Encourage children to show the "Paul and Silas Teach the Jailer That Everyone Can Know Jesus" activity page to their families as a reminder that God's love is for absolutely everyone.

Talk about:

Ask: • Does God love us no matter what color our hair is? Does God love us no matter what kinds of toys we play with? Does God love us whether we're boys or girls, grown-ups or children? Why do you think God love us no matter what?

• How does it make you feel to know that God loves each of us just the way we are?

• Do you know anyone who you can tell about God's love? Who?

Say: God made each of us and loves us just as we are. God loves all people, no matter what they look like, what they do, or what they have. Every person is special to God.

Pray: God, we are so glad to know that you love each of us. Help us to show your love to others, and help them get to know you. We love you, God! In Jesus' name, amen.

"Believe in the Lord Jesus, and you will be saved"
(Acts 16:31a).

We Are Part of God's Family

Romans 8:15-17; Ephesians 3:1-10

What you need:

For each child...
- 1 copy of page 103
- 1 scrap of fabric

You'll also need...
- yarn, and remember to bring your
- Coloring Creations Kit!

What to do:

Write children's names on their pages.

1. Give each child an activity page and two to five crayons. Ask children to hold up their crayons and take turns naming a member of their family for each different color crayon. Allow kids to each tell a friend beside them a few things about the members of their family.

2. Direct children to color the family picture and draw in any other family members that they would like to add. Read the Bible verse, and explain that everyone can be a part of God's family.

3. After children have finished coloring, have them glue pieces of yarn on the people's hair and a scrap of fabric on the baby's blanket.

4. Then direct kids to fold the two top corners of the paper to the back so that there are two small triangles hidden behind the family picture. Next, tell the children to fold the bottom corners of their activity paper to the back so that the bottom of the paper comes to a point.

5. Take the scissors, and show children how to make a small two-inch vertical cut straight down the top middle of the paper.

6. After each child has made this cut on his or her paper, tell the children to fold each of these new corners to the back, pointing toward the first corners they folded. The final two folds should create a point on each side of the cut. The six folds should reveal a heart shape around the family picture. Encourage children to show the "We Are Part of God's Family" activity page to their families as a reminder that God wants everyone to be a part of his family.

Talk about:

Ask: • **Who is in God's family?**

• **How can you show love to other people in God's family?**

Say: **God loves us, and God loves our families. God loves us so much that he wants us all to be part of his family.**

Pray: **Heavenly Father, thank you for making us part of your family. Help us learn to love our family and know that everyone is part of your family. In Jesus' name, amen.**

"I will be a Father to you, and you will be my sons and daughters, says the Lord Almighty"
(2 Corinthians 6:18).

Care for One Another

1 Corinthians 13

What you need:

For each child...

• 1 copy of page 105

You'll also need...

• 1 box of food coloring for every 5 children to share,
• paper towels, and remember to bring your
• Coloring Creations Kit!

What to do:

Write children's names on the pages.

1. Give each child an activity page. Read the Bible verse to children, and point out the child's tears on the activity page. Tell children that God wants us to love and encourage each other. When we feel sad or afraid, our friends can help us feel better. We can also help our friends feel better when our friends are sad. God loves each of us, and God wants us to love each other too.

2. Help each child drop several different colors of food coloring onto the little girl's tears, count slowly to ten, then wipe the tears away with a paper towel. The colors should create a rainbow effect with one firm wipe. Remind kids that when someone cares for us and encourages us, it's as if our tears turn into a beautiful rainbow and we feel better.

3. Encourage kids to finish coloring their activity pages. As children work, remind them that God cares for us just as we can care for our friends.

Encourage the children to show the "Care for One Another" activity page to their families as a reminder that God wants us to love and encourage each other.

Talk about:

Ask: • **When have you felt sad? Why?**

• **How have other people helped you feel better?**

• **How did you feel after they helped you?**

Say: **God wants us to tell him our worries because God cares for us. God wants us to care for each other too. We can love and encourage one another, just as God loves us.**

Pray: **Dear Lord, thank you for caring about us. Help us to help our friends feel better too. In Jesus' name, amen.**

"Let us encourage one another"
(Hebrews 10:25b).

Obey and Serve Your Family

Ephesians 6:1-4

What you need:

For each child...
- 1 copy of page 107
- 5 small, round stickers

You'll also need...
- blank index cards, and remember to bring your
- Coloring Creations Kit!

What to do:

Write children's names on their pages. Cut the index cards into squares that are larger than the stickers, but small enough to fit on the clothing of the girl in the illustration. Keep the backing on the stickers while you cut them apart and separate them from each other.

1. Give each child an activity page and talk about what the girl is doing in the picture. Point out that she is helping her family by setting the table for dinner.

2. Hand each child five different crayons to hold at once. Tell children to draw a big O around the girl in the picture. Read the Bible verse. Hold up a picture and trace your finger around the O as you explain that "O-bey" means to do what you are asked to do.

3. Have children color the rest of the picture and then give each child an index square. Help each child make a pocket on the girl's clothing by taping the sides and bottom of the index square onto the girl in the picture. Give each child five stickers. Remind children when we obey our parents, we show we love them. We don't obey to get stickers or treats. We obey because we love our parents and because God wants us to obey them.

4. Have children put the five stickers into the girl's "pocket." Explain that kids can use the stickers to help them remember to "O-bey." Hold up a sticker and trace your finger around the O.

5. Tell children to take the pictures home, and when they do something their parents ask them to do, they can put a sticker on top of the plate on the table in the picture. When they've obeyed five times, they will have five stickers stuck on top of each other, just as if they were helping the girl in the picture stack the plates on the table!

Talk about:

Ask: • **What are some things your parents ask you to do?**

   • **Why do you obey your parents?**

Say: **God wants us to obey our parents. When we obey our parents, we are showing our love for them and we are serving them. Let's ask God to help us obey our parents.**

Pray: **Lord, help us obey our parents and do what you want us to do. In Jesus' name, amen.**

"Children, obey your parents"
(Ephesians 6:1).

Serve Each Other

1 Peter 4:8-11

What you need:

For each child...
• 1 copy of page 109

You'll also need...
• various scraps of tissue or construction paper in fall colors, and remember to bring your
• Coloring Creations Kit!

What to do:

Write children's names on their pages. Set out construction paper and glue sticks.

1. Hand out the activity pages, and encourage children to color the pages. As children work, ask if anyone would like to tell a story about what is happening in the picture. Allow several children to take turns telling a story about the picture.

2. When children have finished coloring the page, have them cut or tear the fall-colored paper into small pieces to look like leaves.

3. Encourage children to glue the "leaves" onto the paper in big piles. Point out that the two children are working together, cooperatively, to rake the leaves into piles. Talk about how much easier any job is when we help each other.

4. Ask children if they have ever helped someone else do a chore. Have children tear or cut out two or three larger leaves and write or draw on the leaves things they can do to help other people. Instruct kids to glue the larger leaves to the activity page. Encourage children to show the "Serve Each Other" activity page to their families as a reminder that God wants us to serve and help each other.

Talk about:

Ask: • Have you ever had someone help you do a hard job?

• What are some ways you can help someone else?

• How do you feel when someone helps you?

Say: We know Jesus wants us to help people because he tells us so in the Bible. Jesus can help us do things to help others. When we help others, we are sharing God's love.

Pray: Lord, show us ways we can help other people so they will know that you love them. In Jesus' name, amen.

"Serve wholeheartedly, as if you were
serving the Lord, not men"
(Ephesians 6:7).

Indexes

Bible Story Index

Scripture Index

Theme Index